POLISH WING

Robert Gretzyngier
Wojtek Matusiak

MiG-29
'Kościuszko Squadron' Commemorative Scheme

STRATUS

Wydawnictwo STRATUS sp.j.
Po. Box 123, 27-600 Sandomierz 1, Poland
e-mail: office@stratusbooks.pl
www.stratusbooks.com.pl www.mmpbooks.biz

ISBN 978-83-63678-64-7

Authors of MiG-29 photographs: Piotr Abraszek (PA), Peter R. Arnold (PRA), Mark Baczkiewicz (MB), Paweł Bondaryk (PB), Norbert Czajkowski (NCz), Grzegorz Czubski (GCz), Tomasz Gackowski (TG), Robert Gretzyngier (RG), Filip Jereczek-Bambrowicz (FJB), Jarosław Kalemon (JK), Andrzej Ligocki (AL), Wojtek Matusiak (WM), Piotr Michalski (PM), Cezary Piotrowski (CP), Michał Popławski (MP), Andrzej Rogucki (AR), Marek Rogusz (MRo), Miłosz Rusiecki (MRu), Dariusz Węgliński (DW), Wojciech Woźniakowski (WW), Studio LAF/Sławomir Bartosik & Robert Senkowski (LAF), Wojskowe Zakłady Lotnicze nr 2 S.A. (WZL-2).

The decal sheet design is based on drawings prepared by ModelMaker for the repainting of the actual MiG-29s by WZL-2 Bydgoszcz (following the original design of the 'Kościuszko emblem' and pilot portraits by Robert Gretzyngier & Robert Grudzień).

FPHU ModelMaker
ul. Lotnicza 13/2, 78-100 Kołobrzeg
Poland
phone. +48 507-024-077
www.modelmaker.com.pl

MODELMAKER

Decal sheet for MiG-29 aircraft produced by ModelMaker in co-operation with MMPBooks/Stratus

Persons/institutions providing archival photographs: Stanisław Błasiak, Krzysztof Cedrowski, Henryk Chołuj, Kołaczkowski family, Tomasz Kopański, Wojciech Krajewski, Marek Rogusz, Wojciech Sankowski, Piotr Sikora, 23 Baza Lotnictwa Taktycznego (Mińsk Mazowiecki, Poland), Polish Institute and Sikorski Museum (London, UK), Pracownia-Muzeum Arkadego Fiedlera (Puszczykowo, Poland) and the authors.

Dziękujemy Januszowi Piekarczykowi za pomoc w uratowaniu zdjęć!

VOLUNTEERS WHO CONTRIBUTED TO THE COMMEMORATIVE SCHEME PROJECT:

In masking and painting the MiG-29s: Piotr Abraszek, Beata Bartoszewicz, Bolesław Bartoszewicz, Andrzej Bąk, Paweł Bondaryk, Grzegorz Dwórnik, Piotr Hodyra, Marcin Hutny, Paweł Hutny, Monika Idzik, Ewelina Karpiuk, Adam Kostyra, Paweł Leszcz, Andrzej Ligocki, Jasmin Mazloum, Piotr Michalski, Tomasz Obrębski, Paweł Przymusiała, Urszula Rawska, Andrzej Rogucki, Marek Rogusz, Miłosz Rusiecki, Paweł Tuliński, Dariusz Węgliński, Błażej Woszczek, Wojciech Woźniakowski, Grzegorz Zaleski and the authors.

Otherwise: Marek Bazydło, Robert Grudzień, Zbigniew Kuszczyk and the authors.

MOREOVER, A NUMBER OF SERVING MEMBERS OF THE POLISH AIR FORCE HAVE CONTRIBUTED TO THE PROJECT BEYOND THEIR REGULAR DUTIES.

Layout design	Bartłomiej Belcarz
Cover design	Artur Juszczak
Front cover photo	Andrzej Rogucki
DTP	Wojtek Matusiak
	Artur Juszczak
Colour Drawings	Marek Radomski
Stencils	Filip Jareczek-Bambrowicz
Proof-reading	Matthew Willis

Wydawnictwo Diecezjalne i Drukarnia w Sandomierzu
ul. Żeromskiego 4, 27-600 Sandomierz, Poland
phone: +48 15 644 04 00
PRINTED IN POLAND

Includes A3 insert with stencils.

Polska wersja językowa jest dostępna w postaci pliku PDF:
http://stratusbooks.pl/assets/PW21_wkladka_polska.pdf

***Title page:** MiG-29 no. 2960532038, code no. 38 'F/Lt Wojciech Januszewicz', February 2015. ©AR*
***Front cover:** MiG-29 no. 2960532356, code no. 56 'W/Cdr Marian Pisarek', September 2013. ©AR*
***Back cover:** MiG-29 no. 2960535105, code no. 105 'Brig. Gen. Merian Cooper', April 2014. ©AR*

'KOŚCIUSZKO SQUADRON' COMMEMORATIVE SCHEME

The 'Kościuszko badge'

In 1919, one year after WWI ended, Poland was fighting a war on its eastern border, against communist Russia. A group of American flyers, led by Capt. Merian Cooper and Maj. Cedric Fauntleroy, volunteered to join the Polish Air Force. They were posted to an existing unit of the Polish air service, the *7 Eskadra*, and Fauntleroy was appointed to command it. Contrary to a widespread misunderstanding, though, the unit was not formed from scratch by the Americans. In fact it had already logged nearly 200 combat sorties by the time the US pilots joined it.

It is worth remembering that before the USA entered WWI, numerous American volunteers had joined the French Air Force, forming a unit known as *Escadrille de Lafayette*, named after a French general who had fought on the side of the 'colonies' against Britain in the American War of Independence in the 18th century. In a similar way the American-manned unit in the Polish Air Force in 1919 was named after Tadeusz Kościuszko, a Polish general in that war. For the Poles, Kościuszko was seen as a fitting patron for the unit also because he was a distinguished commander during Polish-Russian wars in the late 18th century.

One of the first things the Americans did was to create a badge for the 'Kościuszko Squadron'. The emblem, designed by Lt. Elliott William Chess, used the background of 'Stars and Stripes' and superimposed on it two scythes prepared for fighting (their blades set upright) and a Cracow-region peasant's hat. These were symbols of the Polish campaign against Russia led by Kościuszko in 1794, the first in Poland's history when peasants were not compulsory conscripts but volunteers. The emblem was applied on all aeroplanes of the squadron and metal badges of the same design were worn on uniforms. The

[1] German-designed and Austrian-built Albatros D.III (Oef) fighters of the 7 Eskadra *(the original 'Kościuszko Squadron') at Lwów-Lewandówka aerodrome in December 1919. Aircraft no. I was assigned for the use of Maj. Cedric Fauntleroy.*
[2] A 7 Eskadra *Ansaldo Balilla fighter (Italian design) at Warsaw-Mokotów in the early 1920s.*
[3] A SPAD 61 fighter (French design) of the 'Kościuszko Squadron' (meanwhile renumbered the 121 Eskadra*) at Warsaw-Mokotów airfield in 1926.*
[4] In 1932 the unit (meanwhile renumbered again, now the 111 Eskadra*) was visited at Warsaw-Okęcie by Capt. Edward Corsi, an American pilot of the original 'Kościuszko Squadron'. Here, he is standing fifth from the left (in a dark civilian suit) by one of the unit's French SPAD 51s. Standing at far left is Lt Zdzisław Krasnodębski, who later commanded the 111* Eskadra*, and then No. 303 Squadron.*
[5] A Polish-designed PZL P.7 of the 111 Eskadra *in the mid-1930s.*

[6] PZL P.11c (code no. 5) and P.11a (10) begin a line-up of 111 Eskadra *aircraft, a few months before the outbreak of WWII.*
[7] Hawker Hurricane I no. V6665 RF-J of No. 303 Sqn with the squadron badge below the radio mast.
[8] Close-up of the 'Kościuszko badge' on another Hurricane of the squadron, with the official Battle of Britain score of the squadron chalked next to it. According to RAF Fighter Command No. 303 was the top-scoring unit of the Battle.
[9] Supermarine Spitfire IX no. BS411 RF-I with the squadron badge below the windscreen.
[10] Close-up of the squadron badge on another Spitfire during annual celebrations of the American 'Memorial Day', May 1943.
[11–12] North American Mustang IV KM112 PD-D with the 'Kościuszko badge' on its side. This was the personal mount of the squadron commander: first Bolesław Drobiński, then Witold Łokuciewski.

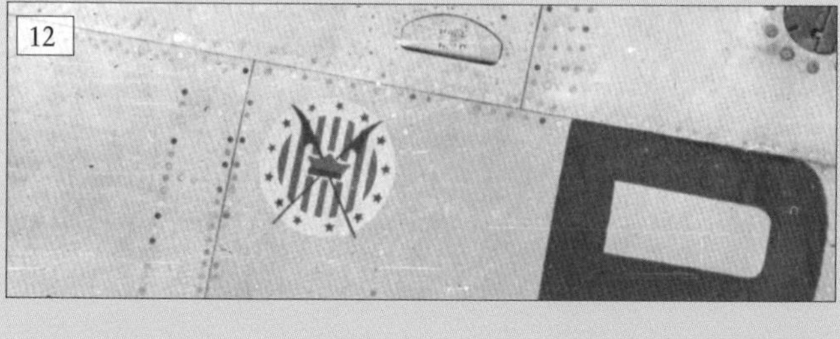

prominent weapons in the badge soon earned it the informal name of 'Kosy' ('Scythes') and the unit's members were nicknamed 'Kosynierzy' ('Scythemen'), a term originally used to describe the 18th century peasant infantry armed with scythes converted for combat.

In the Polish Air Force it is the traditional name that gives a unit its identity. Therefore, the traditions of the unit were maintained regardless of the numberplate that PAF authorities chose to give it, and it has been the 'Kościuszko badge' that established its identity over the next 90 years and more. The same emblem was applied on aircraft of the unit during 1919–1939 in Poland.

When the all-Polish No. 303 Squadron was formed at Northolt during the Battle of Britain, it took on the 'Kościuszko' traditions and the badge was applied on its Hurricanes, Spitfires and then Mustangs throughout the unit's existence (1940–1946).

After WWII Poland was placed under Soviet control, which made it impossible to honour old traditions of military units, especially of those that had fought against communist Russia in 1919–1920.

After the fall of communism, when Poland regained her independence at the beginning of 1990s, the long glorious tradition of the 'Kościuszko Squadron' was revived, and taken on by the *1 eskadra* of the then *1 Pułk Lotnictwa Myśliwskiego* (1 PLM, 1st Fighter Regiment) at Mińsk Mazowiecki near Warsaw. Following reorganisations in the Polish Air Force, today it is inherited by the *23 Baza Lotnictwa Taktycznego* (23 BLT, 23rd Tactical Base) at the same location.

The special scheme

In 2009, to celebrate 90 years of the original 'Kościuszko Squadron' and the forthcoming 70th anniversary of No. 303 Squadron's participation in the Battle of Britain, the back of a MiG-29UB two-seat combat trainer from the unit was adorned with a huge 'Kościuszko badge'. The idea originated from Polish aviation historian Wojtek Matusiak in a conversation with Lt Col. Robert Cierniak, at the time the unit commander at Mińsk Mazowiecki, who supported it enthusiastically. The emblem was designed (based on the original 1919 badge) by Robert Gretzyngier, a renowned aviation historian and artist, and it was applied on the machine by a group of enthusiasts headed by him on 5 June 2009. The following day the aeroplane was the sensation of the annual Góraszka air show near

13

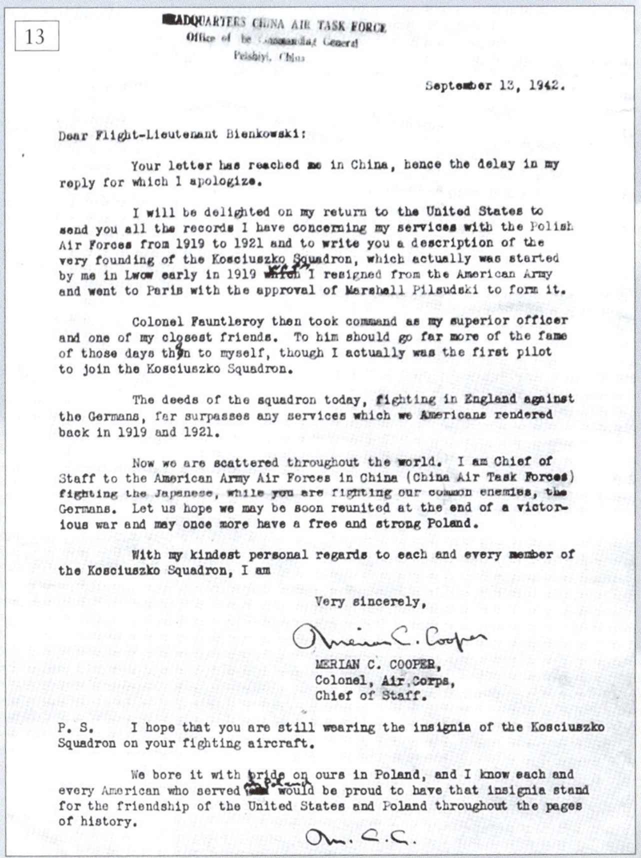

HEADQUARTERS CHINA AIR TASK FORCE
Office of the Commanding General
Peishiyi, China

September 13, 1942.

Dear Flight-Lieutenant Bienkowski:

Your letter has reached me in China, hence the delay in my reply for which I apologize.

I will be delighted on my return to the United States to send you all the records I have concerning my services with the Polish Air Forces from 1919 to 1921 and to write you a description of the very founding of the Kosciuszko Squadron, which actually was started by me in Lwow early in 1919 when I resigned from the American Army and went to Paris with the approval of Marshall Pilsudski to form it.

Colonel Fauntleroy then took command as my superior officer and one of my closest friends. To him should go far more of the fame of those days than to myself, though I actually was the first pilot to join the Kosciuszko Squadron.

The deeds of the squadron today, fighting in England against the Germans, far surpasses any services which we Americans rendered back in 1919 and 1921.

Now we are scattered throughout the world. I am Chief of Staff to the American Army Air Forces in China (China Air Task Forces) fighting the Japanese, while you are fighting our common enemies, the Germans. Let us hope we may be soon reunited at the end of a victorious war and may once more have a free and strong Poland.

With my kindest personal regards to each and every member of the Kosciuszko Squadron, I am

Very sincerely,

Merian C. Cooper

MERIAN C. COOPER,
Colonel, Air Corps,
Chief of Staff.

P. S. I hope that you are still wearing the insignia of the Kosciuszko Squadron on your fighting aircraft.

We bore it with pride on ours in Poland, and I know each and every American who served would be proud to have that insignia stand for the friendship of the United States and Poland throughout the pages of history.

M. C. C.

14

[13] A letter from Merian Cooper sent to No. 303 Squadron in 1942. Note the PS: "I hope that you are still wearing the insignia of the Kosciuszko Squadron on your fighting aircraft. We bore it with pride on ours in Poland".

[14] Famous ace of No. 303 Sqn Witold Urbanowicz (wearing a white hat) with members of the 1 PLM and senior commanders during his visit to Mińsk Mazowiecki air base on 29 August 1995.

[15] The 'Kościuszko badge' as worn on uniforms by unit members: A) the original badge worn in the 7 Eskadra during the Polish-Russian war of 1920; B) the badge of the 111 Eskadra Myśliwska *of the 1930s; C) the badge of No. 303 Squadron in Britain during WWII; D) the patch of the* 1 Eskadra Lotnictwa Taktycznego *introduced on flying suits in the 2000s; E) the low-vis patch of the* 23 Baza Lotnictwa Taktycznego *worn today on field uniforms.*

15

A

B

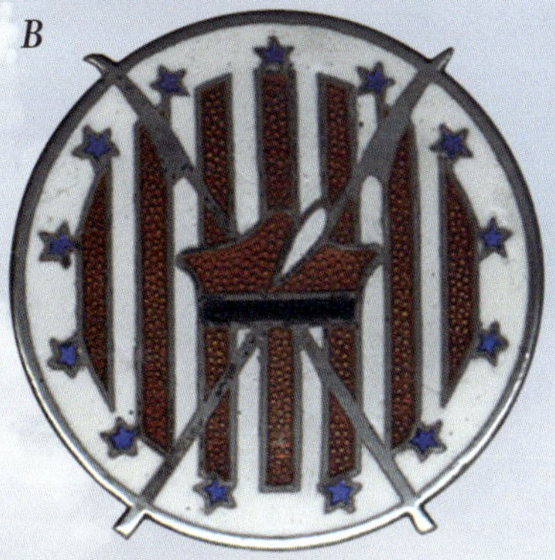

C

D

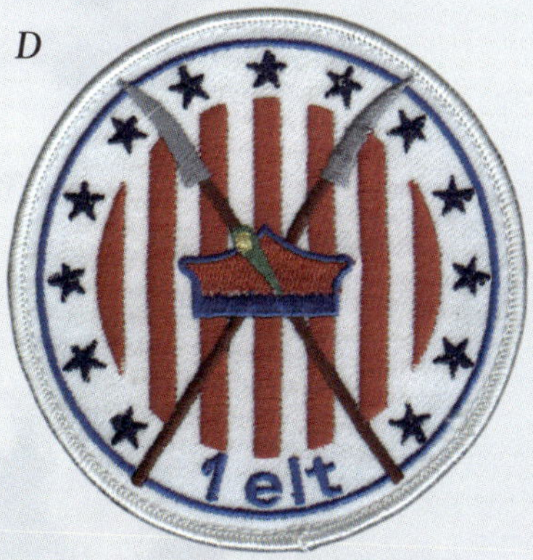

E

16

17

Warsaw. Subsequently it participated in numerous air shows all over Europe.

In 2012 a new commemoration project was initiated by Robert Gretzyngier and Wojtek Matusiak in cooperation with the 23 BLT, now commanded by Col. Maciej Trelka who supported it from the outset. Col. Cierniak, now with the Polish AF HQ, offered help again. A special painting scheme was designed for the unit's MiG-29s. All aircraft would be given low-vis 'Kościuszko badges' on their upper surfaces, and each would be named after an outstanding 'Kościuszko Squadron' pilot from the 20th century wars, and adorned with his portrait. The project became known as 'Kosynierzy Warszawscy' ('Warsaw Scythemen'), reviving the old nickname. A formal application was filed by the Polish Air Force History Foundation and approved by the HQ Polish Air Force. Gen. Lech Majewski, commanding the Polish AF at the time, showed personal interest in the project and supported it.

The entire scheme was to be applied with grey paint so as not to compromise the camouflage effect of the overall finish. Again the design work was done by Robert Gretzyngier, who turned the general idea into detailed drawings of the portraits, based on well-known black-and-white photos, but reduced to just three tones of grey. He created the portraits of all Polish pilots commemorated in the project. Fellow artist Robert Grudzień has prepared the drawings for the four portraits of American officers who originated the 'Kościuszko Squadron' in 1919.

The first three 'commemorative' jets saw their debut during the Open Day air display at Mińsk Mazowiecki on 2 June 2012. Over the next few years all aircraft of the squadron were similarly adorned with portraits of outstanding pilots of the 'Kościuszko Squadron'. All this work was carried out by volunteers.

In 2015 a new camouflage scheme was introduced on Polish MiG-29s, using paler hues of grey. When this scheme was applied during overhauls of aircraft used by the 23 BLT, the portraits and names were reapplied on their fins, as was the 'Kościuszko badge' on their top surfaces.

[16] Wojciech Kołaczkowski, a wartime commander of No. 303 Sqn, in the cockpit of MiG-29 code no. 111 during his visit to the 1 PLM, September 1993. (23 BLT archive)
[17] Ludwik Kraszewski, a veteran of No. 303 Squadron and Lt Col. Robert Cierniak, at the time commanding the 1 Eskadra Lotnictwa Taktycznego, *in front of the latter's personalised MiG-29 no. 115. Mińsk Mazowiecki, August 2007. ©WM*
[18] MiG-29UB code no. 15 adorned with the 10-ft. 'Kościuszko badge', seen during its debut display at Góraszka air show in June 2009, flown by Lt Col. Robert Kozak and Capt. Piotr Iwaszko. ©PRA

18

19

20

[19] MiG-29 code no. 56, with a similar large-size 'Kościuszko badge' on the upper surface, plus portraits and inscriptions commemorating W/Cdr Marian Pisarek, performs at an air show at Stavanger-Sola, Norway, on 9 June 2012. ©AR
[20] MiG-29 code no. 105, commemorating Merian Cooper, the originator of the 'Kościuszko Squadron', photographed in flight during the Baltic Air Policing deployment (code-named 'Orlik' by the Polish AF) to Siauliai, Lithuania in early 2015. This basic colour scheme was standard when the commemorative marking project commenced. Although the shades of grey were the same on all aircraft, the actual disruptive pattern was different on each machine. This is an example of how the upper-surface 'Scythes' were applied in tones of grey on all MiG-29s except single-seater no. 56 and two-seater no. 15. ©PB
[21] MiG-29 code no. 38, commemorating F/Lt Wojciech Januszewicz, photographed in March 2016 at Mińsk Mazowiecki. The code number in dark grey, rather than red, is a first-glance give-away of the new toned-down colour scheme introduced in 2015. ©AR

21

[22] MiG-29 code no. 59 'S/Ldr Henneberg' and MiG-29UB code no. 42 'Col. Fauntleroy' over Mińsk Mazowiecki air base in August 2015. ©PB
[23] MiG-29s nos. 56 'W/Cdr Pisarek' and 40 'W/Cdr Urbanowicz' starring at the Berlin Air Show, September 2012. ©MRu
[24] MiG-29s nos. 115 'F/Lt Gładych' and 111 'F/O Ferić' at Siauliai during the Baltic Air Policing deployment, March 2015. ©PB

[25] MiG-29s nos. 54 'S/Ldr Jankiewicz' and 108 'F/Lt Paszkiewicz' parked on arrival at RAF Fairford for the RIAT, July 2016. ©MB
[26] MiG-29s nos. 38 'F/Lt Januszewicz' and 83 'S/Ldr Łokuciewski' offer direct comparison of their different colour schemes, Mirosławiec air base, May 2016. ©NCz

Zdzisław Krasnodębski commanded the *111 Eskadra* before WWII (1935–1937). In 1940 he formed No. 303 Squadron in Britain and was its first commander until he was shot down and badly burnt in the Battle of Britain. He then held a number of command posts at various levels. He never returned to Poland.

27

[27] MiG-29UB no. 50903014615, code no. 15 was the first aircraft adorned with the huge 'Kościuszko badge' on its upper surfaces. This was done in June 2009 and at the time it was seen as a one-off special scheme. This photo was taken during the air show at Volkel air base, Holland, on 20 June 2009. Note the absence of Polish AF national markings (white-red chequered squares) on wing upper surfaces, as was standard at the time. ©RG

28

[28] In 2012 the aircraft was chosen to commemorate Zdzisław Krasnodębski. By the time this photo was taken over Bydgoszcz in April 2013 the Polish chequered squares had been introduced on wing upper surfaces. ©JK

29

30

31

[29] The 'Mermaid' and the 'Scythes' under the cockpit. Note the blue stencilling and the retouched camouflage. ©WW
[30] The 'Kościuszko badge' was applied here with the original reusable plywood stencils, featuring two stars at the top and three at the bottom (compare photo [47] on p. 13). ©WM
[31] Detail of the 'Cracow hat' in the top surface badge with a red 'eye' in the 'feather' (compare photo [72] on p. 20). ©WM

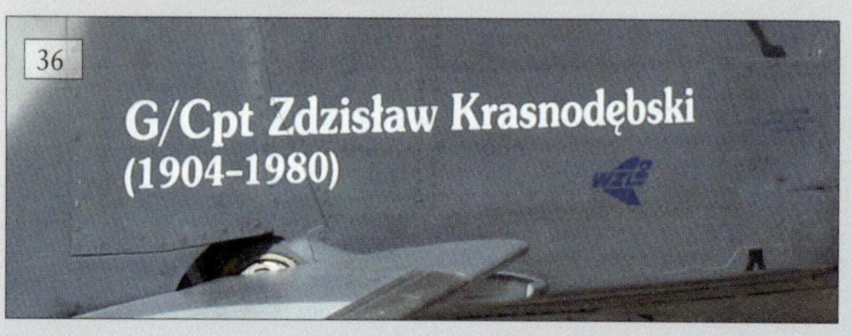

[32,33] The portraits as applied in the last days of May 2012. ©PA, ©PB

[34,35] Polish military ranks are capitalised only at the beginning of a sentence or caption. This resulted in confusion: these were originally capitalised when applied in late May 2012, but within days the spelling was changed. The WZL-2 logo (see p. 80 for details) on the port side was partly obliterated in the process. Note the IV klucz emblem. ©PB, ©PA

[36] The RAF rank inscription on the starboard side involved no such dilemmas. ©MRu

[37] The IV klucz emblem applied on the two-seat MiG-29UBs of the unit. The red devil motif was pun on the name of the klucz (section) commander, Capt. Marcin Boruta, since 'Boruta' is the name of a devil from an old Polish legend. Compare photos [267] on p. 70 and [298] on p. 77. ©PA

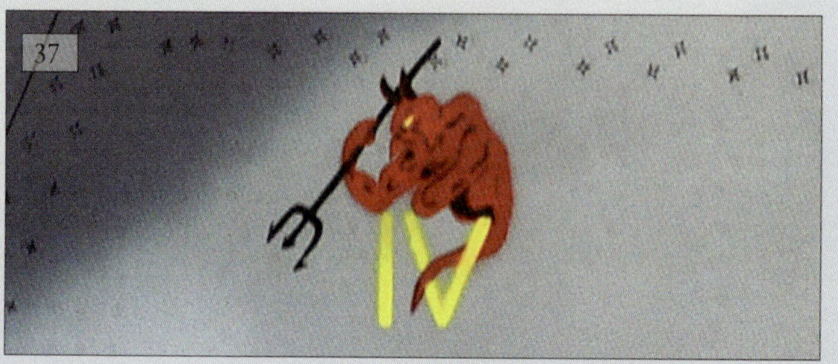

[38,39] MiG-29UB no. 50903014615, code no. 15 'G/Cpt Zdzisław Krasnodębski', 2012.

38

39 [39] MiG-29UB no. 15 during landing run with the brake parachute deployed, Mińsk Mazowiecki, August 2013. ©MRu

40

[40,41] MiG-29UB over Mińsk Mazowiecki base in August 2013. The chequered square markings were applied as standard on wing under surfaces throughout MiG-29 service in Poland. ©PB

41

42

43

44

45
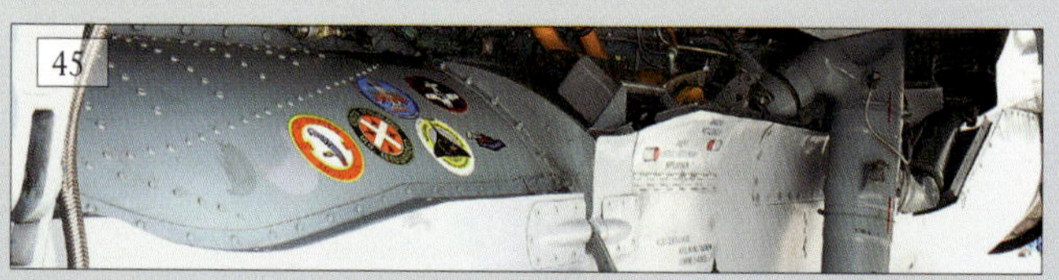

[42,44] The stencil in the starboard main wheel well commemorating 20 years of the MiG-29 in Polish service. ©WM
[43,45] Souvenir stickers from foreign trips inside the port main wheel well as seen in June 2012. ©WW

46

47

[46] In the autumn of 2014 MiG-29UB no. 15 was completely overhauled and repainted at WZL-2 plant in Bydgoszcz. Although the camouflage tones were not changed, the new disruptive pattern was entirely different (compare photo [40] on the facing page). The full-colour 'Kościuszko badge' and the portraits on the fins were reapplied, following the original design. This photo was taken at Mińsk Mazowiecki in February 2015. ©AR

[47] The full-colour 'Kościuszko badge' under the cockpit was also reapplied at WZL-2. Note the three stars at the top and two at the bottom (compare photo [30] on p. 9). ©WM

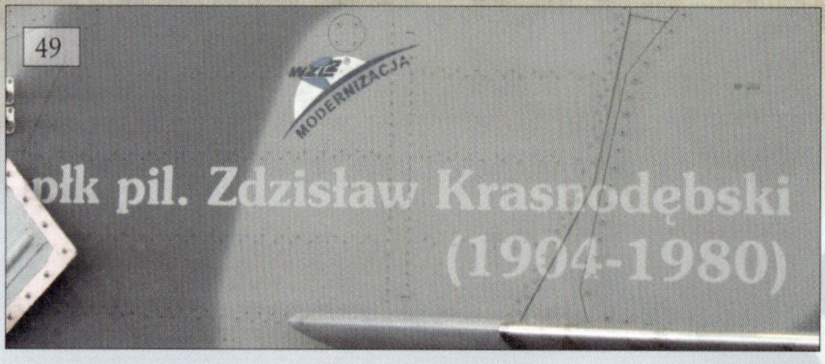

[48] The MiG at Mińsk Mazowiecki in February 2015. ©AR
[49,50] The patron inscriptions were also reapplied and the WZL-2 MODERNISATION logo ([E]) was added on each side. ©WW
[51] When photographed in May 2016, the stencilled note in the starboard main wheel well commemorating 20 years of MiG-29 service in Poland was badly worn (compare photo [42]). ©WM
[52] The port wheel well was still colourful in May 2016, with the souvenir stickers and the WZL-2 greeting stencil on the forward wall (compare photos [43] & [45] on p. 12 and [281] on p. 73). ©WM

Marian Pisarek was an ace, credited with four aerial victories while flying with No. 303 Squadron during 1940 and nine more with other units. Later in the war he commanded No. 308 Squadron Polish AF and then he led the 1st Polish Fighter Wing until his death on operations in April 1942.

[53] MiG-29 code no. 56 was selected as the principal display single-seater, and was adorned with the full-colour 'Kościuszko badge'. On 2 June 2012 it had its public debut during the Open Day at Mińsk Mazowiecki air base, when Lt Col Artur Kałko flew an air display. Note the original version of the upper surface 'Kościuszko badge', identical to that on MiG-29UB no. 15. At the time the aircraft did not carry the Polish AF national markings on upper wing surfaces. ©PA

53

54

[54] The under-wing chequered squares have been present on all MiG-29s throughout their Polish service. The alignment of these insignia varies between aircraft. This shot of no. 56 during the display at RIAT 2012 clearly shows them aligned with the wing trailing edge. ©NCz

[55] By the time this photo was taken in August 2012, no. 56 'W/Cdr Marian Pisarek' had already received the Polish national markings on upper wing surfaces. These were aligned with the aircraft centreline. ©GCz

55

56

[56,57] MiG-29 no. 2960532356, code no. 56 'W/Cdr Marian Pisarek', late 2012.

57

58

[58] Capt. Adrian Rojek performing in MiG-29 no. 56 at the Royal International Air Tattoo, RAF Fairford, 19 July 2015. ©MB
Grey camouflage colours tend to take on different hues depending on the lighting conditions and on the camera/image settings. The same neutral grey may appear bluish, greenish or purplish in various photos, while the appearance of other colours remains natural.

[59] MiG-29 no. 2960532356, code no. 56 'W/Cdr Marian Pisarek', late 2012.

59

[60,61] Portraits of Marian Pisarek applied on the fins of the MiG at the very end of May 2012. ©LAF
[62,63] The name and rank of W/Cdr Pisarek as applied in May 2012. Similar to that on MiG-29UB no. 15, his Polish rank had originally been spelled with a capital 'P', changed to lower case after a few days. Note the old style ([A]) logos of WZL-2. ©MRu, ©LAF
[64,65] The inscriptions on MiG-29 no. 56 photographed in mid-2015. Note the WZL-2 MODERNISATION logo ([E]) applied after the aircraft was upgraded, and the retouched camouflage. ©NCz

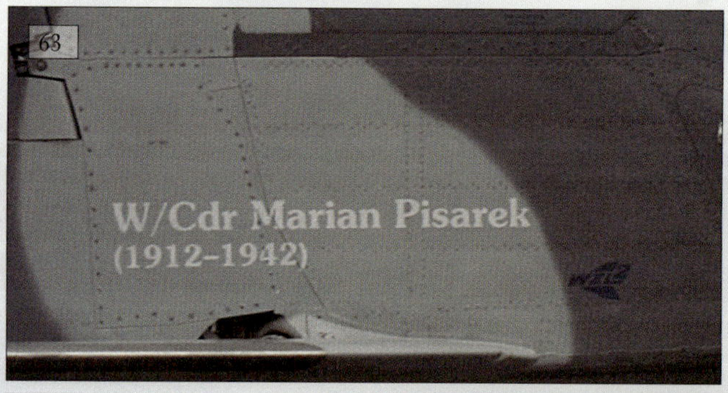

[66,67] Lt Col. Artur Kałko preparing for an air display on 2 June 2012 at Mińsk Mazowiecki air base, the first public display of the MiG-29 no. 56 in the colourful commemorative scheme. The 'Mermaid of Warsaw' (inspired by the coat-of-arms of the City of Warsaw) had been the emblem of the 1 PLM until its disbandment in 2000, applied on both sides of the fuselage, facing forward on each side. It continued to be applied on the MiG-29s of the succeeding units following subsequent reorganisations. This emblem was always applied with the same set of stencils. The 'Kościuszko badge' has only been applied on the port side (the entry to the cockpit), using various stencils. On no. 56 this badge was applied in full colour, with the reusable plywood stencils in use since mid-2000s. ©LAF

[68–70] Despite the colourful display scheme, no. 56 sees normal everyday use with its unit, as shown in these photos taken in August 2012 following a gunnery training sortie. Note the amount of residue from firing the cannon, which covers the port side of the fuselage and reaches well back over the engine housing and nozzle. ©WM

71

72

[71] MiG-29 no. 56 photographed on 9 May 2014 during an air show at Mińsk Mazowiecki commemorating the 15th anniversary of Poland's entry into NATO. Note that by that time the 'eye' of the 'feather' in the 'Kościuszko badge' had been repainted green. ©AR
[72] Close-up of the 'feather' motif, photographed in August 2013, after the 'eye' had been altered from red to green (compare photo [31] on 9). ©WM

MIG-29 STENCILS

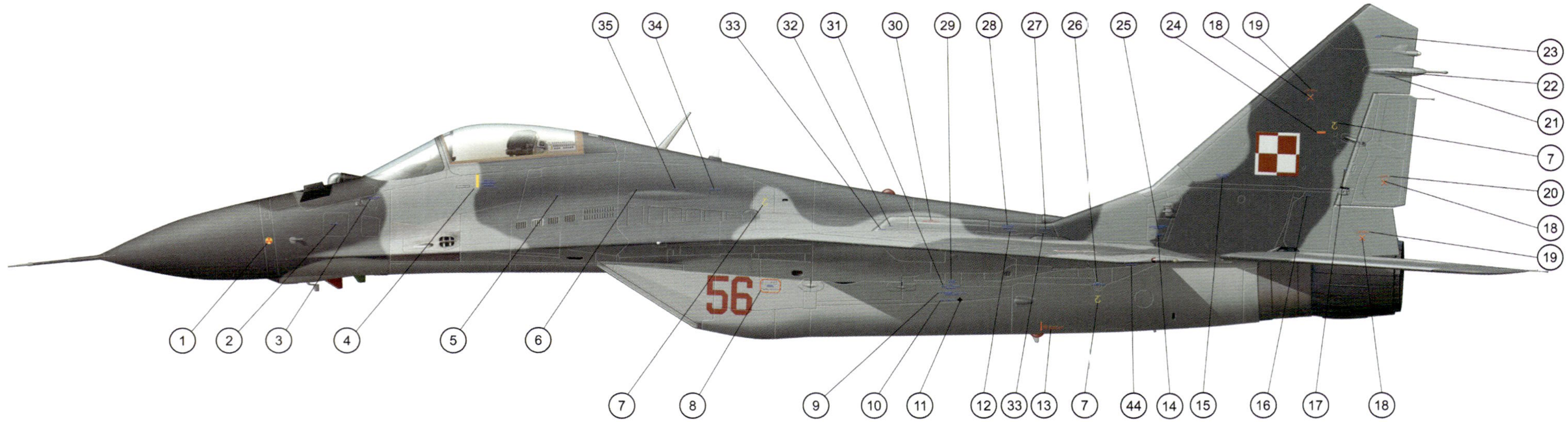

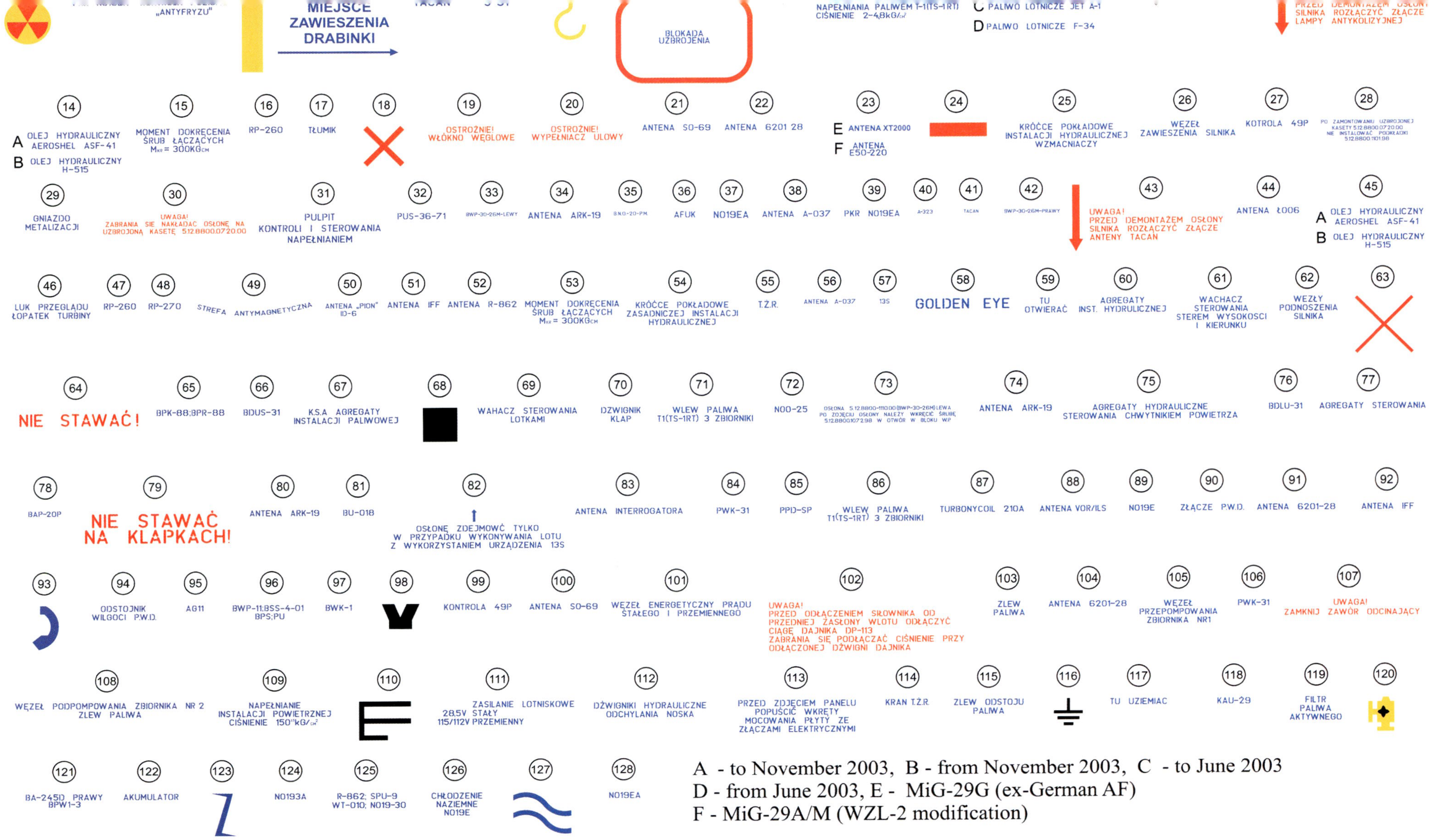

A - to November 2003, B - from November 2003, C - to June 2003
D - from June 2003, E - MiG-29G (ex-German AF)
F - MiG-29A/M (WZL-2 modification)

Stencilling researched and drawn by Filip Jereczek-Bambrowicz ModelMaker, according to original WZL-2 Bydgoszcz documentation.
MiG-29 artwork by Marek Radomski.

128
127
126
56
125
124
100
123
122
44
102
104
121
78
120
11
119
55
120
11
112
113
112
113
112
88
89
90
91
92
93
94
95
96
97
98
99
100
101
44
102
103
104
105
44
106
107
108
109
110
111
112
113
112
113
112
44
119
18
120
11
98
20
115
114
119
118
103
117
116

73

[73] MiG-29 no. 56 photographed in June 2016 during post-overhaul testing at WZL-2. The aircraft was repainted in the new 'pale' camouflage, but the full-colour 'Kościuszko badge' was retained on the upper surfaces. ©JK

74

[74] Also the badge below the cockpit was applied in full colours. The design is a scaled down version of that applied on the upper surface. ©WZL-2

Wojciech Januszewicz was the last commander of the 111 *Eskadra* in September 1939, credited with three or four aerial victories during this campaign. His most epic air combat was fought in defence of his unit's advance landing ground in a lone PZL P.11 against a section of Bf 110s: he downed one of those and chased another away smoking badly, all in full view of his men. Having reached Britain, he then flew with No. 303 Squadron but was killed in combat during the Battle of Britain.

[75] MiG-29 code no. 38 at Mińsk Mazowiecki air base in January 2015. Note the full-colour 'Kościuszko badge' under the cockpit and no other emblem there. ©WM
[76,77] The portraits of F/Lt Januszewicz were applied on the aircraft in early May 2014. The one on the port fin depicts him in typical pre-WWII Polish Air Force flying gear, as he would have appeared during his combats in September 1939 over Poland. ©WW, ©TG
[78,79] The inscriptions on the fins, and the single-tone ([D]) WZL-2 MODERNISATION logo. ©TG

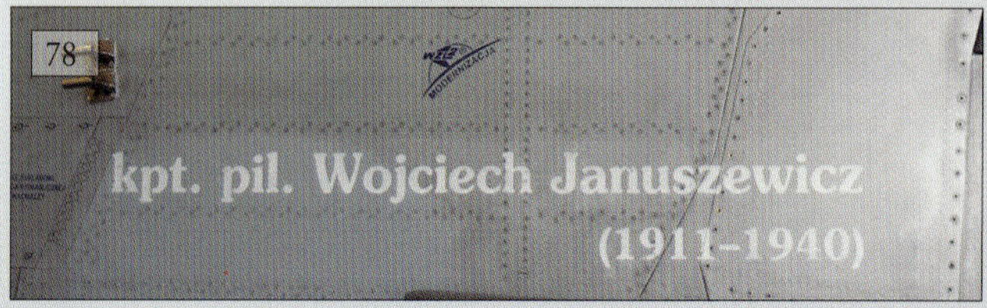

80

[80] The MiG in flight over Mińsk Mazowiecki air base in February 2015, a few weeks after the photo in the previous page. Note the 'Mermaid of Warsaw' under the cockpit on this side. This machine was unusual in that the portraits were painted almost two years after the 'Kościuszko badge' was applied on the top surface in August 2012. ©AR

81

[81] MiG-29 no. 2960532038, code no. 38 'F/Lt Wojciech Januszewicz', early 2015.

[82] At the time the portraits of F/Lt Januszewicz were applied on the MiG in May 2014 it featured both the 'Kościuszko badge' and the 'Mermaid of Warsaw' on the port side. ©WW

[83] The '1000h nalotu' ('1000hrs flying time') stencil on the port intake when the aircraft was still in the 'dark' camouflage. ©WW

[84] 'GOLDEN EYE' stencilled in blue on the housing of the OLS-13S optical seeker head. This stencil is present on MiG-29s of the unit fitted with the improved optical device, although it is hardly visible in most photos. ©WW

[85,86] MiG-29 code no. 38 was the first single-seater repainted in the new toned-down camouflage. These photos were taken in May 2016. ©PB, ©NCz

87

88

89

90

91

92

93
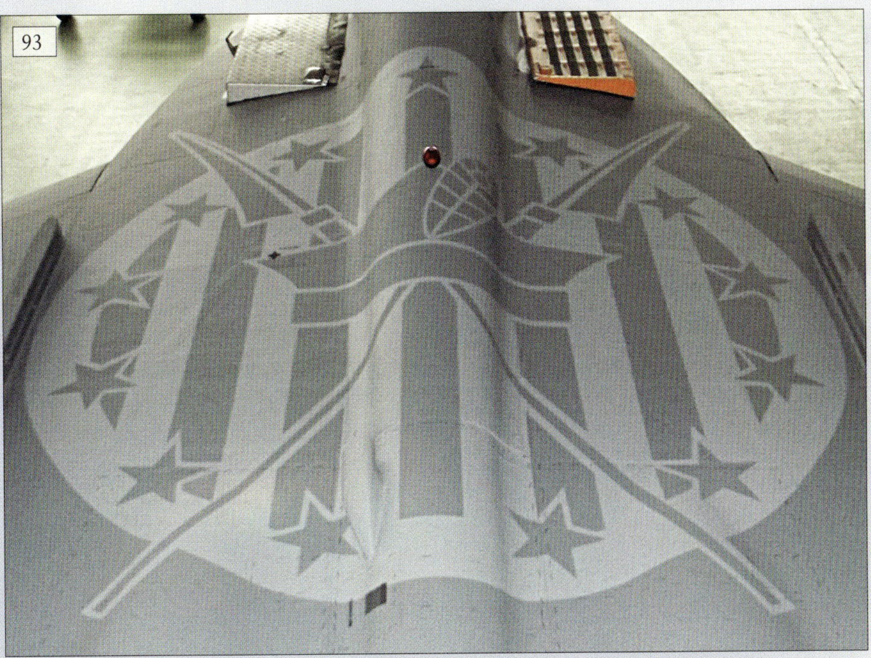

94
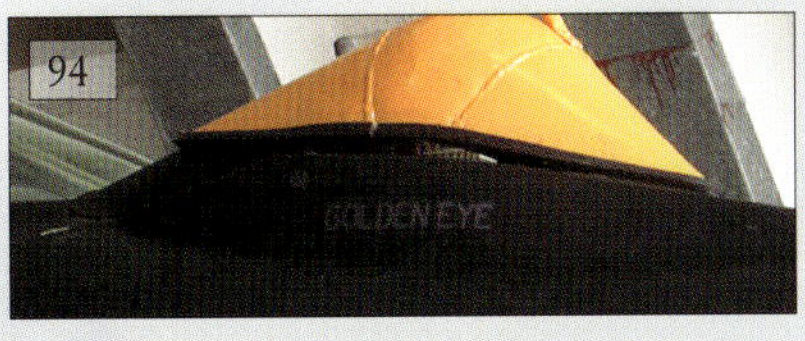

[87,88] Portraits of F/Lt Januszewicz in the new colour scheme. ©FJB
[89,90] The inscriptions and the new ([H]) WZL-2 logos. ©NCz
[91] The badge below the cockpit resembles those applied with old style plywood stencils. ©WM
[92] Innovations of the new scheme include the 'UWAGA WLOT' ('MIND THE INTAKE') stencil and the grey code numbers. ©NCz
[93] The 'Kościuszko badge' on the upper surface. ©FJB
[94] The 'GOLDEN EYE' stencil was also reapplied in grey. ©WM

95

96

97

[97] MiG-29 code no. 38 taking off from Mińsk Mazowiecki air base in April 2016. ©AR

[95,96,98] MiG-29 no. 2960532038, code no. 38 'F/Lt Wojciech Januszewicz', 2016.

98

Witold Urbanowicz was an ace credited with thirteen aerial victories while flying with No. 303 Squadron and four more with other units. He succeeded Krasnodębski as the second Polish commander of the unit. He then led the 1st Polish Fighter Wing when it was formed in 1941. He later fought against the Japanese, the only Polish fighter pilot in combat over China. In the early 1990s he supported reviving the 'Kościuszko Squadron' traditions by the 1 *Pułk Lotnictwa Myśliwskiego* at Mińsk Mazowiecki. In 1996 he was the senior No. 303 Squadron veteran there during a ceremonial hand-over of that unit's trophies and memorabilia to the 1 PLM.

[99] MiG-29 code no. 40 was adorned with the 'Kościuszko badge' on its upper surface and the portraits of W/Cdr Witold Urbanowicz in late July 2012. By that time it already had the Polish AF chequered squares on its upper wing surfaces. The photo taken during an air show at Laage, Germany, on 23 August 2014, shows to advantage the appearance of the all-grey unit badge where it overlaps the camouflage pattern division line, resulting in inverted colours. Note also the distinctive helmet of the pilot, Lt Col. Piotr Iwaszko. ©AR
[100] Lt Col. Iwaszko demonstrates the 'Kościuszko badge' on his flying helmet. ©WM
[101] MiG-29 code no. 40 at Mińsk Mazowiecki air base in August 2015. ©NCz

99

100

101

102

[102] MiG-29 no. 2960532040, code no. 40 'W/Cdr Witold Urbanowicz', 2012.

103

[103] MiG-29 no. 40 at Mińsk Mazowiecki in March 2014. Note that by this time the blue 'wave' of the 'Mermaid' had been truncated during an under-cockpit repaint job and the silver 'Scythes' showed signs of wear. ©AR

104

105

106

107

108
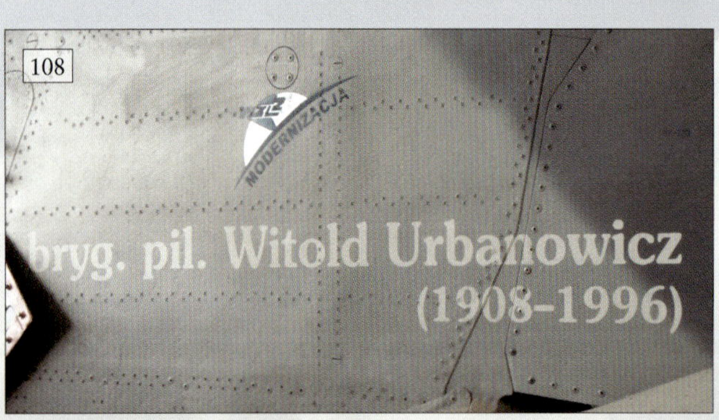

109
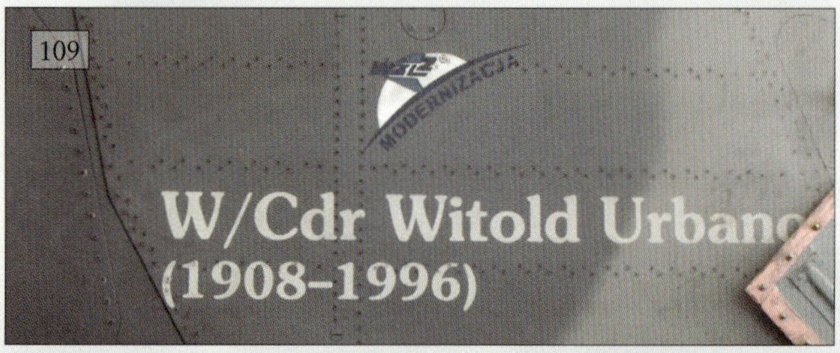

110

[104,105] Portraits of W/Cdr Urbanowicz photographed upon application in July 2012. ©PB, ©WM
[106,107] The inscriptions as they looked when applied in 2012, with the old ([A]) logos of WZL-2. Note that 'gen. bryg.' (generał brygady – *Brigadier General) is a much higher rank than Wing Commander. Urbanowicz was promoted in Poland in retirement, but this did not affect his highest RAF rank (members of the WWII exiled Polish Air Force had temporary or acting RAF ranks according to the Anglo-Polish Military Agreements). ©WM, ©MRu*
[108,109] The inscriptions photographed in 2016, with the WZL-2 MODERNISATION logo ([E]). ©WM
[110] The 'Mermaid of Warsaw' and 'Kościuszko badge' under the cockpit of the MiG. No. 40 was the first aircraft that featured this design of the monotone 'Kościuszko badge' in this position. It was applied using a self-adhesive disposable mask, its design being a scaled down version of that used on the upper surfaces. On this MiG the badge was applied in silver. ©MRu

Jerzy Jankiewicz joined No. 303 Squadron at the beginning of 1941 and then commanded it from July until November 1941 (notably, his three predecessors were all killed on operations when leading the squadron). One of the aerial victories credited to him while flying with No. 303 was perhaps the most important single 'kill' of the Polish AF: a transport aircraft that carried a *Luftwaffe* general and his staff. In 1942 S/Ldr Jankiewicz had the distinction of being the first Polish officer appointed to command a British fighter squadron. He was killed in May 1942 when leading No. 222 Sqn RAF at the head of the North Weald wing on operations over Europe.

111

[111] MiG-29 no. 54 photographed at Gdańsk-Rębiechowo Airport on 30 May 2016. Note what looks like a darker area immediately forward of the portrait on the starboard fin. This patch does not show as such in the upper photo. Clearly, it was finished with paint of different reflectivity. ©CP

[112] MiG-29 no. 54 was the last to have the portraits and name of its patron applied – in late May 2016. This photo was taken in July 2016 at Mińsk Mazowiecki base. Note the condensation streaks across the wings and off the wingtips, revealing the airflow pattern. ©AR

112

[113] MiG-29 no. 2960532354, code no. 54 'S/Ldr Jerzy Jankiewicz', 2016.

113

[114] MiG-29 no. 54 at its home base in July 2016. ©AR

114

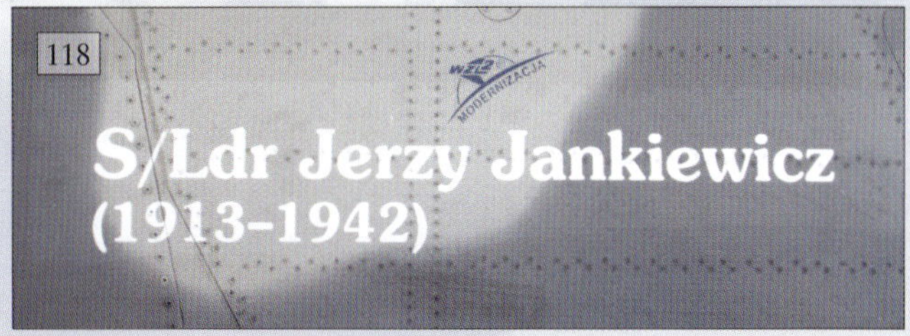

[115–118] Portraits and inscriptions on MiG-29 no. 54 as applied in May 2016. The aircraft featured single-tone WZL-2 MODERNISATION ([D]) logos on the fins at the time. ©WM
[119] The light grey 'Kościuszko badge' below the cockpit. ©WM
[120] The 'GOLDEN EYE' stencil on the optical seeker housing. ©WM
[121] MiG-29 no. 54 on the runway at Mińsk Mazowiecki in July 2016. ©AR

Zdzisław Henneberg was an ace credited with eight aerial victories while flying with No. 303 Squadron. In February 1941 he took command of the unit, and led it until his death on operations in April 1941.

[122] MiG-29 code no. 59 'S/Ldr Zdzisław Henneberg' taking off from Mińsk Mazowiecki in August 2015. The 'Kościuszko badge' was applied on this aircraft in August 2012 and the portraits of the patron in September 2012. Like a number of other MiGs, no. 59 did not feature the 'Mermaid of Warsaw' on either side of the fuselage at the time. ©PB

122

123

124

[123] The 'Kościuszko badge' on the upper surfaces of MiG-29 code no. 59 photographed when it was displayed in the static exhibition during the Open Day at Mińsk Mazowiecki air base on 25 May 2013. ©PB
[124] The badge below the cockpit was applied in silver, further aft than on most other aircraft (compare its position relative to the 'LADDER HANGING LOCATION' stencil and arrow). ©PB
[125] MiG-29s code nos. 59 and 56 about to take off from Mińsk Mazowiecki in August 2013. ©MRu

125

126

[126] MiG-29 no. 2960532359, code no. 59 'S/Ldr Zdzisław Henneberg'.

127

[127] No. 59 photographed over the Alps, returning from the Tactical Leadership Programme training exercise at Albacete, Spain, in March 2013. ©MP

128

129

130
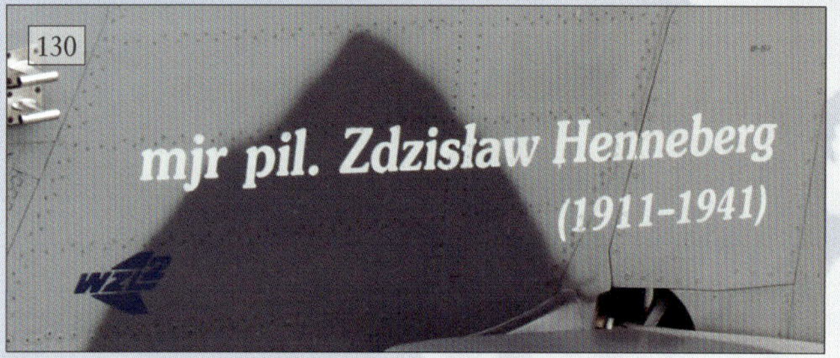

131

132

133

134

135

[128,129] Portraits of S/Ldr Henneberg on the fins. ©NCz, ©WM
[130,131] The inscriptions as originally applied, photographed in May 2013, with old ([A]) WZL-2 logos below. ©PB
[132,133] The inscriptions photographed in November 2014 with the WZL-2 MODERNISATION logos ([F] variant) and prominent traces where the older ones were overpainted. Note how the semi-circular area in the logo on the port fin looks grey at this angle (see p. 80 for details). ©MRo
[134,135] When the aeroplane was photographed in August 2015, the white/silver area was absent in the starboard logo ([G] variant). ©NCz

Wojciech Kołaczkowski joined No. 303 Squadron in late 1940 and then commanded it during 1941–1942. He then led the 1st and 2nd Polish Fighter Wings in Britain during WWII. He stayed in exile after WWII (becoming a professional race car driver). He visited the 1 *Pułk Lotnictwa Myśliwskiego* at Mińsk Mazowiecki on several occasions in the 1990s and helped revive the 'Kościuszko Squadron' traditions there.

His personal Spitfires during WWII were all adorned with the name '*Wojtek*' (a diminutive form of his first name) applied in hand-script style.

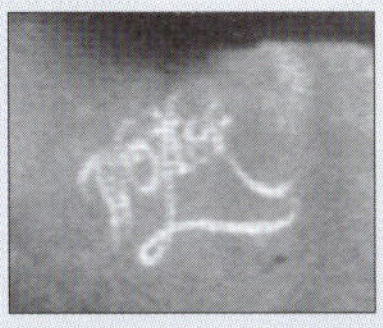

[136] MiG-29 no. 67 at Mińsk Mazowiecki in May 2014. ©WM
[137] The aircraft at the same location in August 2015. ©NCz
[138,139] When photographed in May 2016 the MiG featured a 'Rafale' sticker on the starboard air intake, a souvenir from an air show it had attended. ©WM

136

137

138

139

[140] MiG-29 no. 2960526367, code no. 67 'W/Cdr Wojciech Kołaczkowski', early 2014.

140

141

142

[141,142] MiG-29 no. 2960526367, code no. 67 'W/Cdr Wojciech Kołaczkowski', early 2014.

144

143

[143] The '1000h nalotu' ('1000hrs flying time') stencil on the port intake of the aircraft. ©WM
[144] The MiG taking off from Mińsk Mazowiecki air base in March 2014 with a practice missile on the under-wing hardpoint. At the time it featured both the 'Mermaid' and the 'Scythes' on the port side below the cockpit. ©AR

[145] Top view of the MiG during an air display practice in August 2015. Note the appearance of the 'Kościuszko badge' (applied in early May 2013) with the area of inverted colours on the port side. ©PB
[146] The 'Kościuszko badge' below the cockpit of the aircraft, in light grey. ©WM

145

146

147

[147] MiG-29 no. 67 at Mińsk Mazowiecki in August 2015. Note the 'Kościuszko badge' only below the cockpit. ©NCz
[148] The aircraft at its home base in July 2016, now with 'Wojtek' added on the nose. ©MRu

148

[149,150] Portraits of W/Cdr Kołaczkowski were painted on in mid-May 2013. ©WM, ©NCz
[151,152] The inscriptions as applied in mid-May 2013, above old ([A]) WZL-2 logos. ©WM
[153,154] The same inscriptions in August 2015, with new ([D]) WZL-2 MODERNISATION logos applied elsewhere and older logos obliterated with fresh paint. ©NCz
[155–157] 'Wojtek' in hand-script style (similar to that on Kołaczkowski's personal Spitfires with No. 303 Sqn) was applied on both sides of the nose in May 2016. ©WM

Witold Łokuciewski was an ace credited with eight aerial victories while flying with No. 303 Squadron. In February 1946 he took command of the unit, and led it until its disbandment in December 1946. He returned to Poland after the war. In the wake of the political 'thaw' of 1956 (when the Stalinist communist period ended) he joined the air force, becoming the chief pilot of the Polish AF R&D establishment.

158

159

160

[158,159] The 'Kościuszko badge' was applied on the upper surface of MiG-29 code no. 83 in early May 2014. The unusual patch of camouflage across the centre of the fuselage coupled with somewhat different paint reflectivity gives it a rather unusual appearance. ©AR, ©AL

[160] The badge under the cockpit was applied with light grey paint. ©AL

[161] MiG-29 no. 2960526383, code no. 83 'S/Ldr Witold Łokuciewski'.

161

162

[162] MiG-29 no. 83 landing at Mińsk Mazowiecki air base in May 2016. ©PB

163

164

165

166
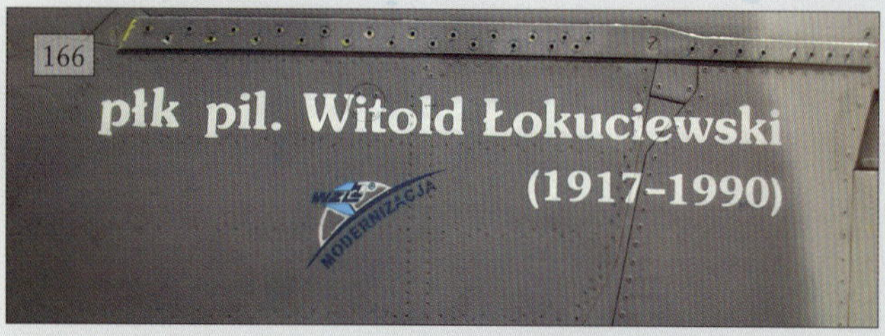

167
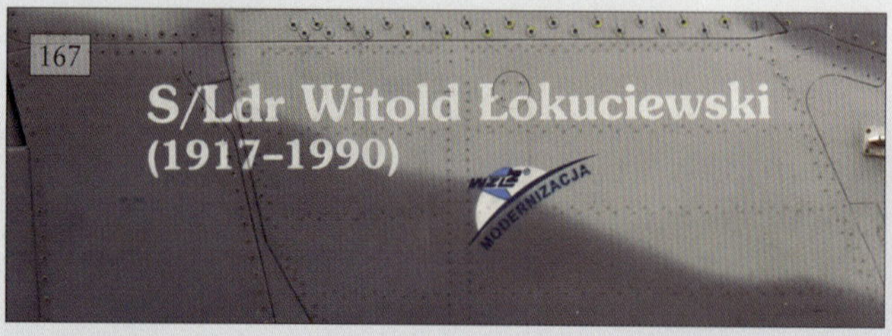

[163] MiG-29 no. 83 at Mińsk Mazowiecki air base in October 2014. ©TG
[164,165] The portraits of S/Ldr Łokuciewski were applied in early May 2014. ©WM
[166,167] The inscriptions on the fins with the WZL-2 MODERNISATION logos ([E]). Most of the white is missing in the port logo ©RG, ©NCz

Bolesław Drobiński was an ace credited with seven confirmed aerial victories while flying with No. 303 Squadron. In 1944 he took command of the unit, and led it until early 1946. He stayed in exile after WWII. In late 1960s he was one of the consultants of the 'Battle of Britain' film and provided some off-screen 'Polish chit-chat' for its soundtrack.

168

[168,169] The portraits of S/Ldr Drobiński were applied on the MiG-29 no. 89 in early May 2014, but the upper surface 'Kościuszko badge' was not applied on this aircraft before it was despatched to WZL-2 for a periodic overhaul (following which it would receive the new lighter grey camouflage scheme). These photos were taken during an air show at Ostrava, Czech Republic, in September 2014. ©AR

169

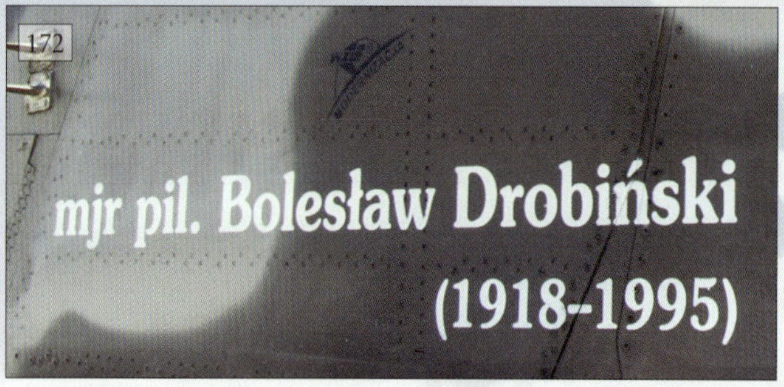

[170,171] The portraits of S/Ldr Drobiński on the tail. ©NCz
[172,173] The inscriptions and the WZL-2 MODERNISATION logos [D]. ©TG, ©NCz
[174] The 'GOLDEN EYE' optical seeker housing stencil. ©WM
[175] The light grey 'Kościuszko badge' below the cockpit. ©AL
[176] MiG-29 no. 89 during pre-flight preparations in May 2014. Note the air-to-air training missile on the under-wing pylon. ©TG

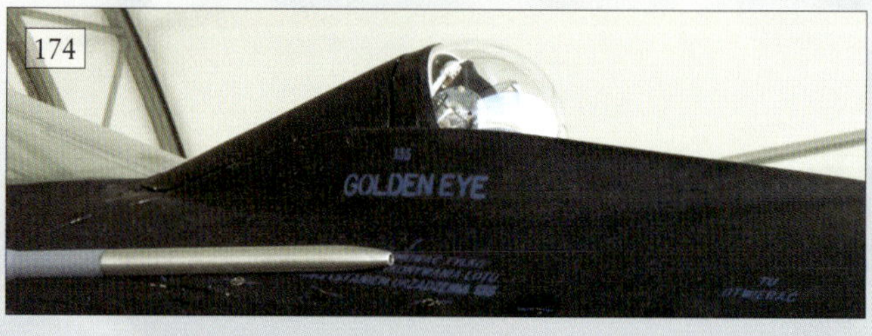

177

[177] MiG-29 no. 2960526389, code no. 89 'S/Ldr Bolesław Drobiński'.

178

[178] MiG-29 no. 89 taking off from Mińsk Mazowiecki base in October 2014. ©AR

Merian Cooper co-founded the American volunteer unit with the Polish Air Force in 1919 and in 1920 he was appointed the second American commander of the 7 *Eskadra* (after Fauntleroy). Shot down and captured by the Russians, he only avoided being executed by concealing his identity. He then managed to escape and reached Polish territory. Cooper subsequently became a successful film producer in the USA, authoring the original 'King-Kong' in 1933. In 1952 he was awarded an Academy Award, which makes him, as far as can be ascertained, the only fighter leader in history to win an 'Oscar'.

179

180

[179] MiG-29 code no. 105 during flying practice over Mińsk Mazowiecki air base in late April 2014. Note that the Polish national markings are aligned with the wing trailing edge. The aircraft is flown by Lt Col. Iwaszko, in his distinctive helmet. ©AR

[180] The MiG at its home base in early January 2015, during preparations for the Baltic Air Policing deployment to Siauliai, Lithuania. Note the missiles on under-wing hardpoints. ©WM

181

182

183

184

[181,182] The portraits were applied on the MiG in early July 2013. ©WM, ©WW
[183,184] MiG-29 no. 105 and Merian Cooper suffered from a serious blunder (either gremlin subversion or the great adventurer himself having fun from beyond the grave!). When stencils were prepared for application of the inscriptions, the life dates of Gustaw Sidorowicz (see MiG-29UB no. 28 on p. 70) were somehow mistakenly applied for Merian Cooper. The mistake was not discovered until the MiG became the star of the static display during Radom Air Show in August 2013, seen and photographed by thousands of the public. If really born in 1905 Cooper would certainly have been the youngest squadron commander in 1920! Note the old ([A]) WZL-2 logos. ©MRu, ©PB
[185] Within days the correct dates were applied. ©WM
[186] When photographed in May 2014 the MiG sported the WZL-2 MODERNISATION ([E]) logos. ©WM
[187,188] Another set of WZL-2 logos, of the latest [H] style, was seen on the aircraft in May 2016. ©NCz

185

186

187

188

[189] MiG-29 no. 2960535105, code no. 105 'Brig. Gen. Merian Cooper'.

189

190

[190,192] MiG-29 code no. 105 'Brig. Gen. Merian Cooper' on patrol during the Baltic Air Policing deployment to Siauliai, Lithuania, March 2015. A single missile under each wing was a standard weapon fit on normal sorties. ©PB
[191] The 'Kościuszko badge' below the cockpit was applied in silver on this aircraft. ©WW

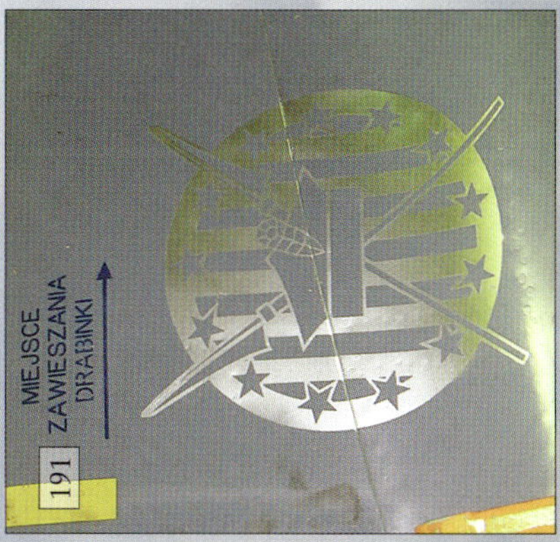

191

192

Ludwik Paszkiewicz was an ace credited with six aerial victories while flying with No. 303 Squadron. His 'kill' during a training sortie on 30 August 1940 was the first victory credited to No. 303 Squadron (and was immortalised in a famous sequence in the 'Battle of Britain' film). He was killed in combat during the Battle of Britain.

[193] The 'Kościuszko badge' was applied in silver below the cockpit of no. 108, as on several other MiGs. ©WW
[194] The badge on the upper surface, though, was unlike that of any other aircraft of the unit. It was applied (in May 2013) as a 'negative' of the standard form seen on other machines. ©AR

193

194

195

196

[195] MiG-29 code no. 108 at Mińsk Mazowiecki air base in early January 2015, during final preparations for the Baltic Air Policing deployment to Siauliai, Lithuania. Note the missiles on under-wing hardpoints. ©WM
[196] The MiG photographed in March 2015 at Siauliai during the Baltic deployment. Note the single missile under each wing: a standard armament during routine patrols. ©PB

197
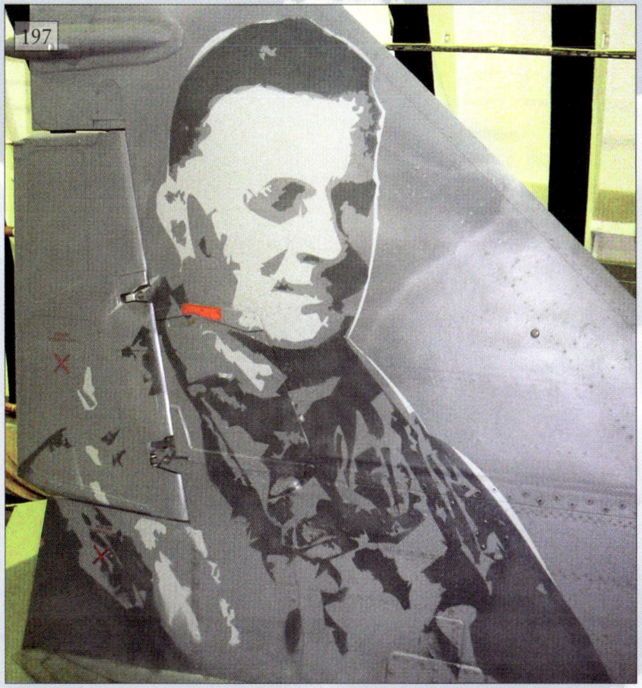

198

199

200

201

202

[197,198] The portraits were applied on this aircraft in early May 2013. ©WW
[199,200] When the inscriptions were applied in May 2013, the aircraft sported the interim ([B]) logos of WZL-2. ©WW, ©PM
[201,202] By the end of 2014 the upgrade of the MiG was shown by the relevant WZL-2 MODERNISATION ([E]) logos. These were applied using 'silvery' paint (see p. 80). ©WM
[203,204] Unlike with the previous Baltic Air Policing missions, the 2015 one was not commemorated with special emblems on the fins. However, a sticker identifying the 'Polish Military Contingent Orlik-6', as the deployment was known officially, was applied in the port wheel well of the MiG. Note also the unusual shape of the digit 8 in the code number, different from those on other MiGs. ©WM

203

204

[205,206] MiG-29 no. 2960535108, code no. 108 'F/Lt Ludwik Paszkiewicz'.

205

206

207

[207] MiG-29 code no. 108 on patrol from Siauliai, Lithuania, during the Baltic Air Policing deployment, March 2015. ©PB

[208] MiG-29 no. 2960535108, code no. 108 'F/Lt Ludwik Paszkiewicz'.

208

Mirosław Ferić was an ace credited with ten aerial victories while flying with the 111 *Eskadra* and No. 303 Squadron. He was killed in a flying accident in February 1942. His personal diary evolved into the informal chronicle of No. 303 Squadron and was continued by his colleagues until 1946.

[209,211] MiG-29 no. 111 was the first aircraft painted in the low-vis scheme of the 'Warsaw Scythemen' project. The badge on upper surfaces and the portraits were applied in the last days of May 2012 and on 2 June 2012 Capt. Adrian Rojek gave a flying display in this MiG (when these photos were taken). Note the absence of the Polish AF chequered squares on wing upper surfaces. ©PB, ©PA

209

210

[210] A month later the MiG (along with no. 56) was a star of the Royal International Air Tattoo at Fairford, UK. This appearance involved a particularly moving moment when the Polish servicemen met Philip Methuen-Feric, the son of Mirosław Ferić, who never knew his father, being born just a few months before his death. ©NCz

211

[212] MiG-29 no. 2960535111, code no. 111 'F/O Mirosław Ferić'.

212

213

[213] A few weeks later, on 27 August 2012, Philip Methuen-Feric and Witold Urbanowicz Jr (the son of another outstanding pilot of No. 303 Squadron) visited Mińsk Mazowiecki air base. This photograph in front of no. 111 shows them with the unit pilots. Left to right: Lt Rafał Kowaleczko, Sub-Lt Kamil Rola, Capt. Grzegorz Czubski, Lt Michał Popławski, Lt Col. Antoni Czerniec, Capt. Jan Kaczor, Maj. Artur Piskorz, Philip Methuen-Feric, Col. Maciej Trelka (commanding 23 BLT), Witold Urbanowicz Jr, Maj. Piotr Iwaszko, Lt Marcin Łękawa, Lt Bartosz Kida, Capt. Cezary Lesiński, Sub-Lt Jacek Stolarek, Lt Col. Artur Kałko, Capt. Paweł Czajka. Note the Polish chequered squares now applied on wing upper surfaces. ©WM

214

215

[214] Capt. Grzegorz Czubski in the cockpit of MiG-29 no. 111 in August 2012. This pilot's commitment to promoting the 'Kościuszko Squadron' traditions of his unit has played an important part in starting the project. The 'Kościuszko badge' below the cockpit of this aircraft was applied with the old plywood stencils (note the two stars at the top), but grey paint was used, to match the monotone 'Scythes' on the upper surface. ©WM

[215] The MiG photographed during air display practice in April 2014. This was the first aircraft with the all-grey badge on the back. The tip of the left 'scythe' that extended into a lighter grey field was applied in darker grey, introducing the 'colour inversion' principle, which was then applied to a much larger extent on some other aircraft. The painting of the top-side 'Scythes' was completed on 26 May 2012. ©AR

216

217

218

[216,217] The portraits of F/O Ferić were completed on 30 May 2012 as the first ones in the whole project. ©RG, ©WM
[218] Similar to MiGs nos. 15 and 56, the Polish rank of F/O Ferić was originally capitalised. Note the [A] WZL-2 logo. ©WM
[219] Within a few days the initial 'P' was changed to lower case, and the WZL-2 logo was partly obscured. ©LAF
[220] The inscription on the starboard fin photographed in the evening on 26 May 2012. ©WM
[221,222] By May 2014 the MiG displayed the new [D] WZL-2 MODERNISATION logos. ©WM

219

220

221

222

223

224

225

226

227

[223,224] No. 111 is one of a number of MiGs, on which the portraits were at some point affected by engineering work on the fins. ©MRu

[225,228] MiG-29 no. 111 at home in July 2016. Note the altered camouflage pattern on outer fin surfaces (compare photos [209] & [211] on p. 56). ©WM, ©MRu

[226,227] A NATO AWACS souvenir sticker was applied during the Berlin Air Show in May 2016 (a similar sticker was also applied in the same position on MiG no. 105). ©WM

228

Eugeniusz Horbaczewski was an ace, credited with three aerial victories while flying with No. 303 Squadron during 1941–1942, and then fourteen more with other units. In 1943 he commanded No. 43 Sqn RAF and was then scheduled to take command of No. 303 Sqn, but a grave illness prevented this. After recovery, in 1944 he took command of No. 315 Squadron instead, but was killed on operations in August.

[229] Both the portraits and the top-side 'Kościuszko badge' were applied on MiG-29 code no. 114 in the first days of May 2013. A couple of weeks later it was photographed, towed behind a standard military truck at Mińsk Mazowiecki base. ©WM

229

230

[230,231] On 10 May 2014 the MiG was shown in the static display during the Open Day at Mińsk Mazowiecki air base when the 15th anniversary of Poland's NATO membership was celebrated. On this occasion the aircraft had an unusual combination of under-wing stores, with four launchers for unguided rockets and two air-to-air combat training missiles. ©PB, ©MRu

231

232

233

[232] MiG-29 no. 114 during air display practice in August 2015. The upper surface scheme of the aircraft is easily recognised by the light grey area on the port wing shaped like a 'clenched fist'. ©PB
[233] The MiG taking off during an exercise deployment to Mirosławiec in May 2016. ©NCz
[234] MiG-29 no. 114 taxiing at Mińsk Mazowiecki base in May 2014. ©WM

234

[235] MiG-29 no. 2960535114, code no. 114 'S/Ldr Eugeniusz Horbaczewski'.

235

236 [236] MiG-29 no. 114 landing at Mińsk Mazowiecki base in July 2015. ©TG

237

238

239

240

241

242

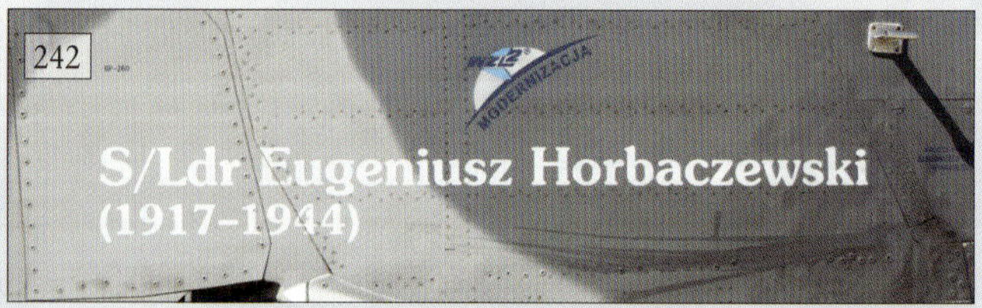

243

244

[237,238] The portraits on the MiG photographed in May 2014. ©MRo, ©MRu
[239,240] The inscriptions as applied in 2013, with the special WZL-2 logo commemorating 15 years of MiG-29 overhauls there ([C]). ©PM, ©PB
[241,242] By May 2014 the WZL-2 MODERNISATION logos ([E]) were applied, to record the upgrade of the MiG. ©NCz
[243] The monotone 'Kościuszko badge' as applied below the cockpit in May 2013. ©MRu
[244] At some point between mid-2014 and mid-2015 the badge was reapplied in a different form. ©NCz

Bolesław Gładych was an ace, credited with five aerial victories while flying with No. 303 Squadron during 1941–1942 and then twelve more with other units. During 1944–1945 he gained special fame while flying with the 56th Fighter Group USAAF (notably, he continued to wear proudly his No. 303 Sqn 'Kościuszko badge' during that period). After WWII he settled in the USA. He died on 12 July 2011 as the last Polish fighter ace of WWII.

[245] MiG-29 no. 115 takes off from its home base in August 2015. ©NCz

245

246

247

[246,247] During the Open Day at Mińsk Mazowiecki air base on 25 May 2013 no. 115 was displayed with three air-to-air missiles under each wing. ©PB

[249] The 'Kościuszko badge' under the cockpit of the MiG. ©WM
[250] MiG-29 no. 115 touches down at Mińsk Mazowiecki in August 2013. ©MRu

[248] MiG-29 no. 2960535115, code no. 115 'F/Lt Bolesław Gładych'.

248

249

250

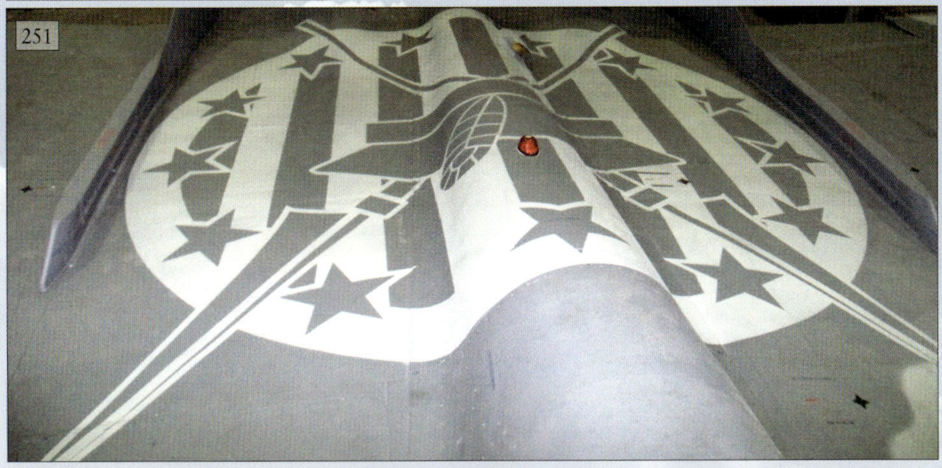

[251] The 'Scythes' on the upper surface of MiG-29 no. 115 were applied in mid-August 2012. ©WM
[252,253] The portraits were applied in in late October 2012. ©WM
[254,255] The inscriptions as applied in October 2012, and [A] WZL-2 logos. ©MRu
[256,257] By the end of 2014 the MiG had undergone upgrade work at WZL-2, as shown by the new [E] MODERNISATION logos. ©NCz

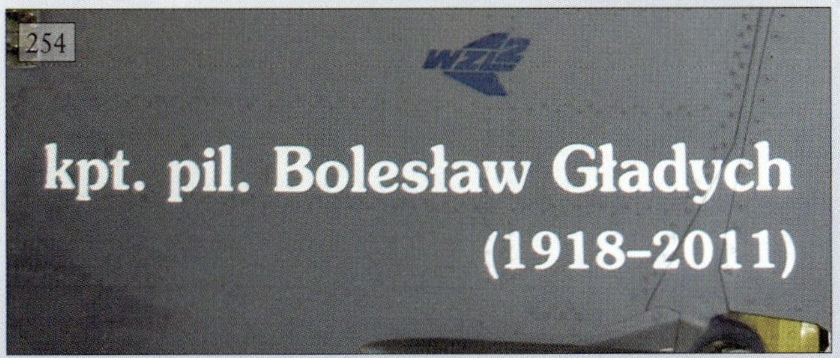

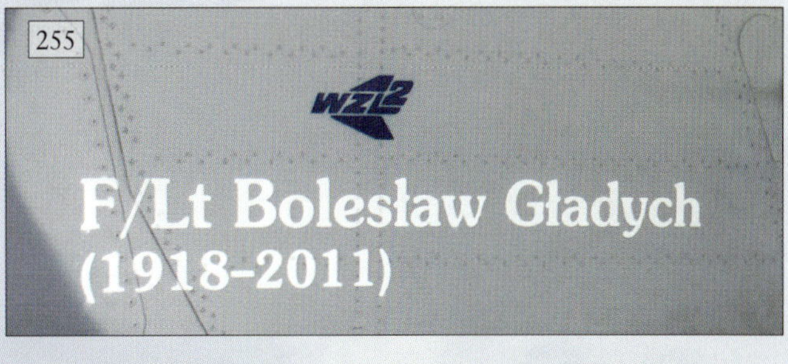

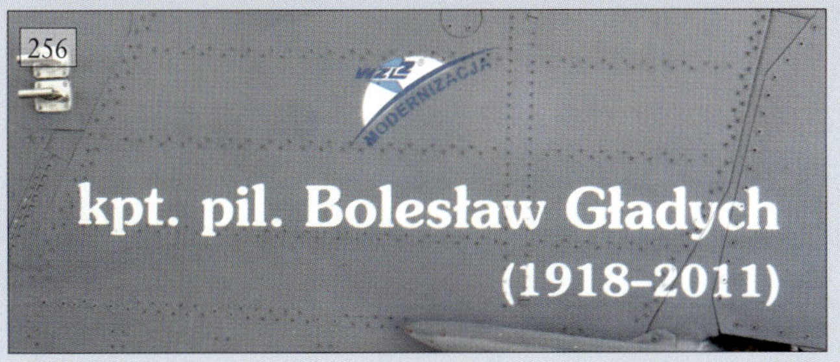

Gustaw Sidorowicz commanded the 111 *Eskadra* at the outbreak of WWII in 1939. Seriously wounded in air combat on the first day of the war, he then stayed in occupied Poland and served with distinction with the Polish underground resistance movement (including a successful escape when arrested by the Gestapo). In 1944 he was instrumental in preparing landings of an RAF Dakota in occupied Poland to pick up agents and components of the V2 missile captured by Polish resistance. In 1990 he visited the 1 *Pułk Lotnictwa Myśliwskiego* at Mińsk Mazowiecki, encouraging the revival and continuation of the 'Kościuszko Squadron' traditions there.

258

[258,259] MiG-29UB code no. 28 upon application of the portraits and the 'Kościuszko badge' on top surface in early May 2013. ©PB
[260] During the farewell ceremony of the Baltic Air Policing contingent on 8 January 2015 no. 28 was part of the static exhibition. For the occasion the aircraft carried six air-to-air missiles on wing hardpoints. Note the new [E] WZL-2 MODERNISATION logo at the base of the fin. ©WM

259

260

261

[261] MiG-29UB no. 50903014528, code no. 28 'Lt Col. Gustaw Sidorowicz'.

262

[262] MiG-29UB code no. 28 'Lt Col. Gustaw Sidorowicz' as backdrop for the guard of honour with the 23 BLT colours. ©WM

263

264

265

266
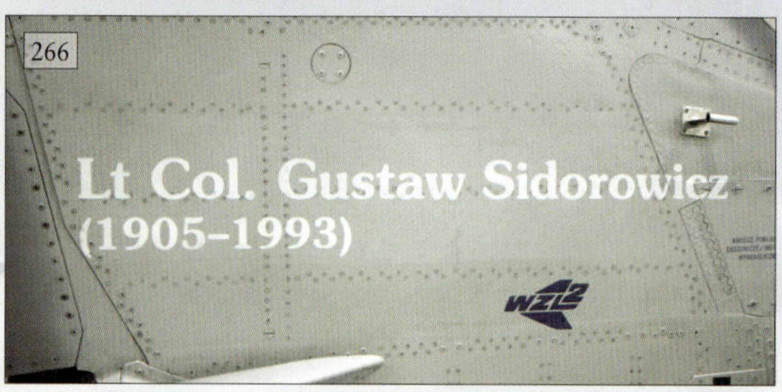

[263,264] The portraits were applied on MiG-29UB no. 28 in late April 2013. ©AL, ©PB
[265,266] The inscriptions were applied in early May 2013. Since Gustaw Sidorowicz never served outside Poland, and consequently he never had any RAF or USAAF rank, his Polish AF rank was translated to English for the starboard inscription. Note the original ([A]) WZL-2 logos. ©JK, ©PB
[267] The emblem of the IV klucz. MiG-29UB no. 15 featured the emblem in an almost identical form [compare photos [37] on p. 10 and [298] on p. 77]). ©WM
[268] The 'Mermaid of Warsaw' and the full colour 'Kościuszko badge' applied on the port side below the cockpit. ©JK
[269] The greetings from WZL-2 staff (left) and the commemoration of the 20th anniversary of the MiG-29 in Polish service stencilled in the port main wheel well (compare photos [278] & [279] on p. 73). ©AL

267
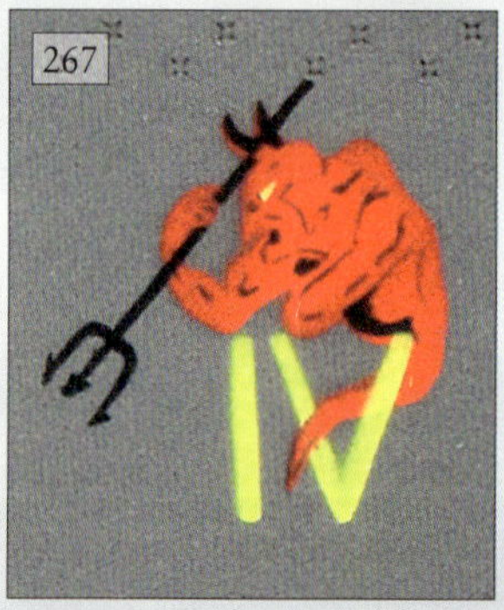

268

269

270

[270] *The 'Kościuszko badge' was first applied on the upper surface of MiG-29UB code no. 28 in early May 2013. ©PB*

[271] *The top-side badge after the MiG was repainted in the new toned-down finish (as the first aircraft of the type). ©NCz*

[272] *MiG-29UB code no. 28 at Mińsk Mazowiecki base in May 2016. ©WM*

271

272

273

[273] MiG-29UB during a test flight from Bydgoszcz in December 2015, after it was repainted in the new scheme at WZL-2 there. ©JK
[274] MiG-29UB code no. 28 back in service with its unit in May 2016. ©NCz
[275] MiG-29UB taxiing at Mińsk Mazowiecki in August 2016. ©WM

274

275

276

277

278
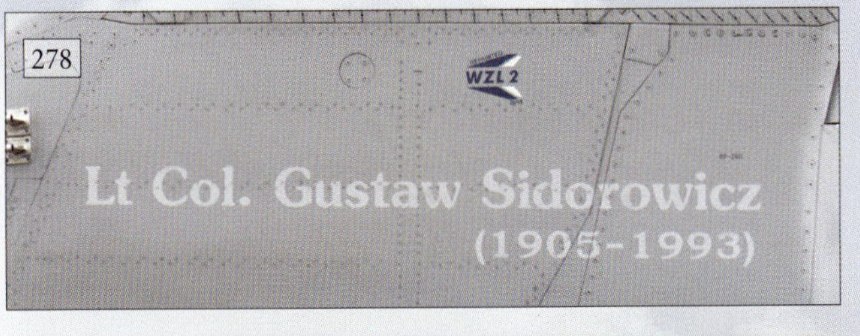

279

280

[276,277] When the portraits were reapplied in the new colour scheme, their positions were reversed, the one showing Sidorowicz in full flying gear now on the port fin and rudder. ©WM
[278] The inscriptions were also switched between the fins, the English one now being on the port side. This was accompanied by the WZL-2 REPAINTED 2015 logo ([J]). ©NCz
[279] The starboard inscription with the Polish rank and the latest WZL-2 MODERNISATION logo above it ([I]). ©NCz
[280] The code number and the intake warning sign. ©WM
[281] The greetings from WZL-2 staff on the front wall of the port main wheel well. ©WM
[282] The stencil applied for the 20th anniversary of the MiG-29 in Polish service still present in the port main wheel well. ©WM
[283] The monochrome 'Kościuszko badge' was applied at the WZL-2 in a similar style to those originally painted on with plywood stencils. ©WM

281
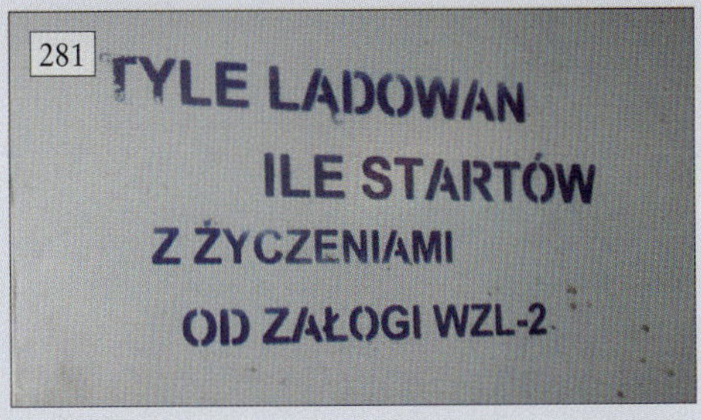

282

283
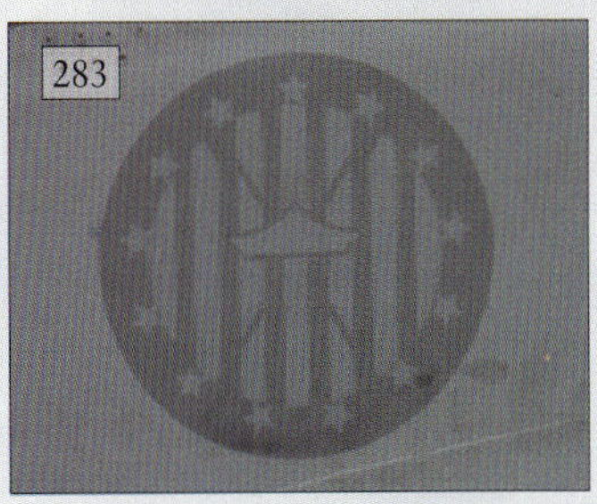

Cedric Fauntleroy was the first commander of the 'Kościuszko Squadron': he co-founded the American volunteer unit with the Polish Air Force in 1919 and was appointed the first American commander of the 7 *Eskadra*. He led it until June 1920, when he was promoted to command a group of eskadras, which included his previous unit. He commanded these during the Russian cavalry's advance on the city of Lwów in mid-August. This was probably the first ever successful defence of a major city by air units in the virtual absence of defending army troops. After cessation of hostilities in Poland he returned to the USA in 1921.

284

[284] MiG-29UB code no. 42 'Col. Cedric Fauntleroy' at Mińsk Mazowiecki air base in May 2014. ©WM, ©PB
[285,286] The MiG landing at the same base in July 2015. A number of differences can be spotted in the aircraft finish, including the retouched camouflage under the cockpit and on the wing leading edge, the altered WZL-2 logo on the fin and the stencilling below the cockpit re-applied in blue (compare photos [290] & [291] on p. 76). ©TG

285

286

[287] MiG-29UB no. 50903014642, code no. 42 'Col. Cedric Fauntleroy'.

[288] MiG-29 no. 115 touches down at Mińsk Mazowiecki in August 2013. ©MRu

[289] The 'Kościuszko badge' below the cockpit when it was painted on in early May 2013. On this MiG it was applied in dark grey. ©DW
[290] The 'Mermaid' and the 'Scythes' in May 2015. Both the 'Kościuszko badge' and the red stencilling were partly obliterated before May 2014, and after a while the stencilling between the two emblems was re-applied in blue (compare photos [285] & [286] on p. 74). ©NCz
[291] The 'Kościuszko badge' was applied on the upper surface of this aircraft in early May 2013. It had an unusual form due to the complicated camouflage pattern on the central fuselage. ©PB

289

290

291

292

293

294

295

296

297
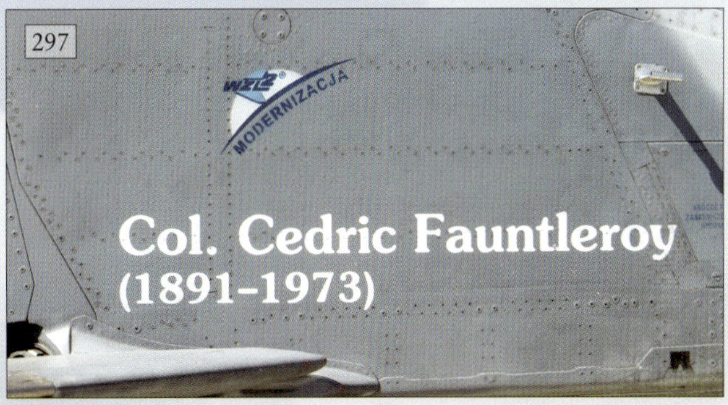

298

[292,293] The portraits as applied on MiG no. 42 at the end of June 2013. ©NCz
[294] The original inscriptions applied in 2013. The last characters of the inscription on the port side were soon partly obscured with a patch of new paint, as shown in this photo from early 2014. Col. Fauntleroy's life dates were based on several publications, but one was later found incorrect and amended (see photos [305,306] on p. 79). ©AR
[295] The inscription on the starboard side upon application in June 2013. Note the [A] WZL-2 logo. ©AR
[296] Later a larger patch of new paint completely obliterated the ending of the port inscription, which was reapplied by hand without any stencils, resulting in a rather non-standard form of the last characters in both rows. This photo was taken in August 2015, by which time the WZL-2 MODERNISATION logo ([E]) had been applied. ©NCz
[297] The starboard inscription remained unaltered, although the old WZL-2 logo was replaced with the new MODERNISATION one. ©NCz
[298] 'Boruta the Devil' of the IV klucz on the fin of MiG-29UB no. 42 was somewhat different from that on nos. 15 and 28 (compare photos [37] on p. 10 & [267] on p. 70). ©NCz

299

[299] MiG-29UB no. 42 in the new paint scheme, photographed at WZL-2 works airfield in Bydgoszcz in June 2016. ©JK

[300–302] MiG-29UB no. 42 at Mińsk Mazowiecki air base in July 2016. ©WM, ©MRu(2)

300

301

302

303

304

305

306

[303,304] The portraits in the new scheme. ©WM, ©NCz
[305,306] The inscriptions, as corrected in August 2016, and the new WZL-2 logos ([H] variant). ©WM
[307] The 'Kościuszko badge' on upper surface. ©WM
[308] The 'Kościuszko badge' below the cockpit, similar to the one applied on the MiG before repainting. ©NCz
[309] The code number in grey with a different style '4', and the intake warning note. ©NCz
[310] The greetings from WZL-2 staff in the port main wheel well were also applied in grey. ©WM

307

308

309

310

311

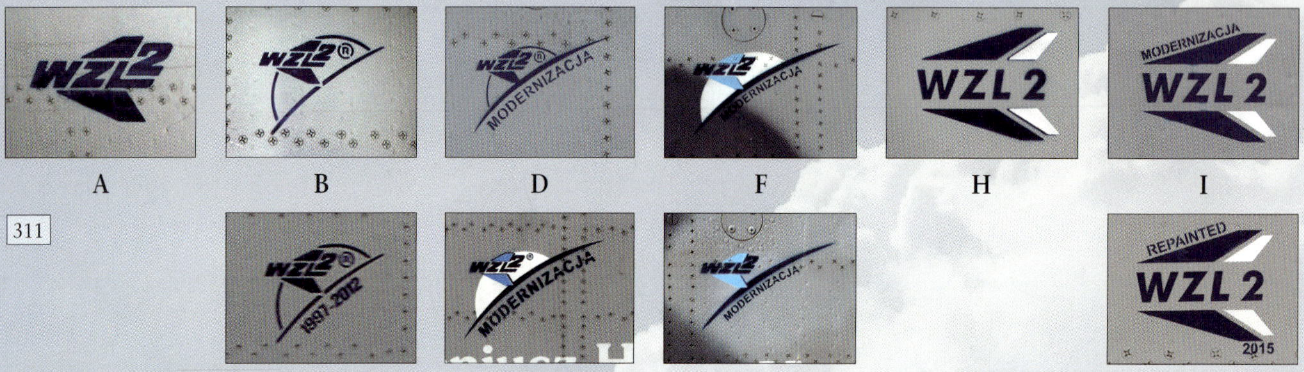

312

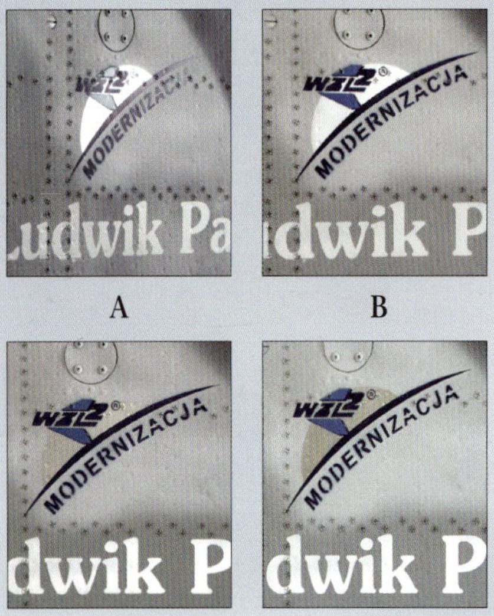

[311] WZL-2 logo variants seen on MiG-29s between 2012 and 2016:
[A] The older variant used until 2012. ©WM
[B] The altered variant introduced in 2012. ©WM
[C] As [B] but with the dates '1997–2012' to mark 15 years of MiG-29 overhauls at WZL-2. ©PM
[D] As [B] but with the word 'MODERNIZACJA' (MODERNISATION), applied on upgraded MiGs. ©NCz
[E] As [D] but in three tones (with the half-disc either flat white or silvery white). ©NCz
[F] As [E] but the word 'MODERNIZACJA' smaller. ©NCz
[G] As [F] but without the white area. ©NCz
[H] Completely new logo design, introduced in 2015. ©NCz
[I] As [H] but with the word 'MODERNIZACJA'. ©NCz
[J] As [H] but with the word 'REPAINTED' and year number. ©NCz
[312] Four photos of the WZL-2 MODERNISATION logo ([E] variant) on MiG-29 no. 108 taken on one occasion, showing how the 'silver' variant of the logo may vary in appearance from white to relatively dark grey depending on the viewing/lighting angle. ©WM

313

[313] MiG-29UB no. 28 with logo [I], MiG-29 no. 111 with logo [D] and MiG-29 no. 114 with logo [E] photographed at Mińsk Mazowiecki air base in May 2016. ©WM